Luzy Lessons

LEARNINGS FROM A
WILD ALASKAN SLED DOG

WENDY BATTINO

WENDY BATTINO
LIVE YOUR ADVENTURE

wendybattino.com

Luzy Lessons: Learnings From a Wild Alaskan Sled Dog

Wendy Battino ©2017

ISBN: 978-0-692-88903-9

Library of Congress Control Number: 2017941959

Photographs, stories, and tools by Wendy Battino

Published by: Wendy Battino, Live Your Adventure

Copy Editors: Bonnie Schreiber Burt, Ellen Wolf, Laura Wright, and my Mom

Designer: Michelle Radomski, OneVoiceCan.com

Printed in the USA

To order single or bulk quantities online go to www.wendybattino.com. (Retail discounts are available for bulk orders.)

For Luzy

Inside you will find:

Foreword by Lisbet Skogen Norris
3-time Iditarod Finisher

Introduction

Luzy Lessons & Stories

Luzy Tools

About the Author

Thank you Rick and inspired
family, friends, and tribemates.

Foreword

I would never recommend a husky as a pet. They are independent natured, they cannot be trusted off-leash, they can be wild and destructive.

BUT

They speak to your soul. They are intuitive beings. They are a conduit to the wilderness.

This is a book about a husky. This is also a book about soul sisters.

I used to be afraid of the dark. Who knows what's out there? With my dog team, I feel safe. If there is wild-life around, they know. When they catch that whiff of wilderness, they charge. My senses are expanded. I am keyed into the environment in a way I can only be with the dogs.

I love the night now. One of my greatest pleasures in life is traveling with my dog team under the light of a full moon. Everything sparkles. Crisp moon shadows flit past. Miles, too. In especially magical moments, aurora shimmers overhead. Here, I find bliss. My huskies and I have a symbiotic relationship that defines my being, fills my heart and gives me meaning in life. Together we cross mountain ranges, run down vast river ways, cross ancient portages, traverse coastal spits. We learn from each other.

I love their independent natures, their unwavering desire to run, their thick coats and almond shaped eyes. Their individualities. Oh man, their individualities. Part of the satisfaction of training and conditioning a team for a long distance race like Iditarod is the practice of bonding, managing, and solidifying a cohort of wild, feisty, focused, shy, and loving personalities into a cohesive working unit—Victor is feisty; Nils hates running next to him, Sunshine is oblivious to his snarling, Vinnie snaps back, Svidd avoids his gaze, Barkly engages with a roar—and that's just one possible pairing in a team of sixteen strong! It's addicting and it feeds the soul. We travel together, we eat together, we rest together. We are partners.

In Luzy's crystal gaze, I recognize my Ruby. Ruby is my soul sister. She has taken me to Nome, a thousand miles across Alaska, twice. Everything I have accomplished, that I am proud of, I have done with Ruby. She is a real lead dog; she is my inspiration. No matter the weather, time of day, whether we have gone five or five hundred miles, she jumps up and is ready to hit the trail. This is special. She is special.

Wendy is Luzy's soul sister.

Wendy is dynamic and kind. She is a teacher, in the truest and most compassionate sense of the word. At heart I think she may be as wild as her Luzy—she walks with bears; sleeps in their nests. She snowshoes across mountain ranges; skis through the heart of Alaska's wildest areas. She is strong, intuitive, and I am constantly struck by the lessons she interprets from the natural world and from her animals—Luzy in particular.

This book is a reflection of that wonderful, complex, loving relationship. It is full of wisdom about self love, appreciating nature, being present and authentic—lessons Wendy has divined from her time with life/self/nature-loving Luzy.

My advice—take them to heart!

Much love,

Lisbet Skogen Norris, 3-time Iditarod Finisher
Owner/Guide at Arctic Dog Adventure Co., Fairbanks, Alaska
www.arcticdogco.com

The Alaskan Husky

Luzy is an Alaskan husky, a type of dog bred specifically for their desire to run and pull. Alaskan huskies are technically "mutts"—a healthy mix of Siberian husky, malemute, Irish setter, border collies, hounds—basically anything someone thought might improve speed and endurance while dogsledding. As a result, huskies are some of the most elite athletes on the planet. They can easily run a hundred miles a day. They are uniquely adapted to thrive in sub-Arctic winter conditions. They have incredible metabolisms that allow them to instantly convert food to fuel, a phenomenon still not completely understood by scientists. They come in all shapes, sizes, and colors. The one thing that unites them is an incredible desire to pull. Sled dogs do not need to be taught to pull; they do it instinctively. It is quite remarkable, much like Luzy herself!

Rise Above, Look Down, Smile.

Introduction

Hi there, I am Wendy. I live in Alaska in the log home I built with my dear husband, Rick, in a land that inspires me. I would like you to meet my mentor, Luzy. She came to me during a transition in my life when I wanted more time in deeper connection with the glorious natural world of Alaska and I wanted to share this connection with others. Luzy looked me in the eye and simply said, "Let's go!"

I first met Luzy when I borrowed her for a winter expedition in 2013. Anja, a neighbor and talented dog musher, drives a team of fantastic Alaskan huskies and Luzy was a part of her pack. At the time, Luzy was three years old and wild and goofy, fun-loving and smart, and maybe too smart. She would not follow directions unless it suited her. Luzy bewitched me into taking her home and she still has me wrapped around her paw. She has warm glacier eyes that look into you and learn how to bend you to her will. She is a Jedi. She is also an Alaskan husky sled dog, who is now my skijor partner. Skijoring is like mushing but the musher is on skis, and it is a BLAST. We do expedition skijoring and explore far into the wilderness. Luzy can pull a 70 pound sled 30 miles all by herself in one day and not get tired. She is my soul sister, personal comedian, wise woman, and mischievous-crazy guru. Like any good friend, she is constantly teaching me.

I also have a Labrador, a brand new husky, and two cats who are all very special. You may see them peeking out of some of the photos. I love them dearly.

The first time I met Luzy it took me ten minutes to get a harness on her because she was all bubbling energy and power. She bounded around like a wolf-kitten and kicked me in the face leaving a welt down my cheek, then licked me and gazed into my eyes with her baby blues. She was crazed with excitement to run. I fell completely in love. It was like I was reunited with a part of myself. When the harness was on we took off like cartoon characters with our tongues hanging out.

Luzy knows her own worth. She knows how to charm those around her and right away I could see she was in love with life, and loved herself, too. They say huskies are close to the wolf. They have a strong sense of self, of wilderness and relationship to others. It is a powerful thing this self-worth. It is a grown-up relationship you have with huskies. You do not "control" them, you earn their respect and hope they want the same things you do, because then you get to fly together.

Luzy and I have skijored over 1,000 miles across the Alaskan landscape, sleeping under the Northern Lights and breathing in the trees. In summer, we paddleboard and hike and swim. She knows when I am going to fall before I do, and when I want to go Gee or Haw

(sled dog for right and left). I trust her, admire her, and laugh a lot around her. Sometimes I laugh-groan. Like the time she leapt out of the car window, while we were moving, to chase a baby moose. She didn't get the moose and finally came back to me.

I have taken most of these photos on my iPhone while running to catch up with Luzy's antics and wisdom. This book came to be because every being is sacred. It is time we humans recognize and celebrate that we are not alone, that we are not the only smart beings and that, in fact, we can learn from all forms of life here on our glorious planet. I also honor sled dogs and Alaska, where we cherish our connection to nature.

This book of lessons learned from Luzy is for all of you who have connected to the magic of animals, or want to. You know the brilliance of your own animal friends and together we can celebrate this sacred knowing.

Let me know what you think! I would love to hear from you about your own animal connections and what you think of Luzy. Do you want further guidance on any of Luzy's Lessons? I coach how to bring these lessons into your everyday life. You can reach me at www.wendybattino.com.

Know that you are awesome.

Live your

own adventure.

Venture into your wild and trust yourself.

You deserve a grand life.

You belong in the driver's seat.

Luzy has locked me out of the car so many times I think she does it on purpose.

Abundance mindset. It works.

Seconds
after Luzy
ate my
sandwich.

Wake up!

Who is Training Who?

She claims the house and us as hers now. We have come a long way from our early days together. The first time I tried to invite Luzy inside, she careened against walls and bashed into windows. I spent three months working with her to sleep in my tent in the yard before trying the house again. The first night, she ripped through the tent wall to chase our cat. I sewed up the tent and we tried it again. Month one in the tent, she stood guard all night staring at me. Month two, she lay down and watched me all night. She began to lie back to back with me. She sang a soft, lilting wheeze while she slept. One day, she chose to walk into the house. She leapt to the top of the fridge and ran around the countertops. I tied her to our seven-foot couch and she tried to drag it down the stairs.

Luzy is always ready to GO. In the first 30 days with her, I got a fat lip, sprained ankle, broken bicycle, and bruises everywhere from trying to keep up with her.

Today, Luzy is "tame"; she has finally trained me. She realizes how fragile I am and is gentler on me. We can both appear presentable, but, if we get a whiff of woods, our wild comes out to play.

Go ahead, bask for a moment today.

Be wacky.

It feels good to move.

Enjoy naps.

13

Be unabashedly you.

You are
a big deal.

Explore your world.

Eat
real food
with gusto.

Skijor Bonanza

After 150 miles and seven days out on the trail, Luzy, friends, and I skijored off the Yukon River and into the village of Tanana. Bedlam ensued. You see, the villagers had stacks of dried salmon and bundles of fish on racks outside their homes. Their own dog teams were safely tied out. To our dogs, it was the supermarket of their dreams. There was no controlling them. I noticed Laura and our other friends zig zagging down the main street from one fish pile to the next, but they managed to keep their dogs OFF the piles. Luzy? Fuggedaboutit.

She dragged her dog partner, Chewy, the sled, and me directly to the first pile of salmon she saw and proceeded to lay into those frozen fish with pure gusto, the sled on its side and Chewy looking bewildered with me yelling my head off and trying to get Luzy off the fish. It was embarrassing, and I knew disrespectful as these fish were crucial food for the village's own dogs to survive through winter. What an entrance. I finally got my team under control and we trudged down the rest of main street, my head hanging about as low as Luzy's full belly. Friendly villagers came out and waved, seeming to know all about us already. We had a wonderful stay in Tanana, and Luzy drooled the entire time.

Rest up for the next adventure.

A caribou skin
will do nicely.

18

Be here now.
This is your power.

Claim it.

Make yourself
comfortable,
you belong here.

Me: Get off
the couch!

Luzy: ...

We are elemental.

**Enjoy
being
you.**

**Share your stuff
with newcomers.**

23

Understand one another.

Luzy and the Veterinarian

Approaching Luzy's posterior with a thermometer is not advisable. It started nicely enough with a sweet welcome from the vet in California, where we had been vacationing for the past month. The veterinarian was going to check Luzy out and give us a health certificate to fly home to Alaska.

And then. Pandemonium.

The vet, a vet tech, and I could not convince Luzy it was okay. That thermometer only got within two feet of Luzy and the ear-piercing howling began. The vet dropped the thermometer, Luzy barred her formidable teeth, and then she was so out of there. I still don't know how she got out the closed door, but I was running down the surgery hall after her with the vet and tech following close behind. We passed a cute dachshund who began barking and thinking he should take Luzy's cue and make a break for it. Then there was a very un-amused Siamese cat on a table. I finally caught up to Luzy in the waiting room where she had two gorgeous giant poodles cowering in the corner. Their owner was wide-eyed looking from White Fang to me and the vets who had come tumbling into the room. Luzy alternately glared at the front door willing it to open and snarled at the poor poodles. I got hold of Luzy who sweetly licked my hand and then snarled again at the general assembly. I looked to the vet who motioned me out. We were done here. The kind veterinarian came out to the car with the signed paperwork. Luzy was good to fly.

Chill with friends.

Never question your looks.

Or your smell.

Go to the mountains and learn from them.

You
are
nature.

Soak
it
all
in.

Have you played today?

Know that magic surrounds you.

When Life Sucks, You are Still Awesome

No matter how bad you feel, you are awesome.

One summer, Luzy was doing her usual, sprinting full force through the woods when she caught a splinter in her shin, and it embedded there. She didn't let on anything was bothering her but she limped—badly. She needed minor surgery; they found a piece of wood in her, got it out, stitched her and gave her a splint. Now, this girl likes to move. I was miserable anticipating her frustration. But you know what? She just went with it calmly and majestically. She let herself be in pain.

Two weeks later...

She still had the splint and she was still limping when she leapt out of my car window in the middle of our little village and burst into the Talkeetna Roadhouse. She smelled bacon.

I ran in just in time to see a tourist giving her a slice off his plate. She walked back to the car with me with her head high.

So, go after what you want right now! Whatever would make you feel better, you deserve it.

In this photo, Luzy is on meds, out of it, in pain, can't walk and look at her! There is no doubt she is a powerful force. This is how I see YOU. This is the real you. Take care and I love you.

Friends
are
important.

Get close
to the
Earth.

Listen
with love.

Look to where you want to go.

37

Mind meld.

You get to live with animals.

Remember... You are an animal.

Please yourself!

(Because you can't
please everybody.)

Anchorage International

It is my fault in the first place. I am tired.

Nineteen hours after starting our journey home, we make it into Anchorage. There is Luzy in her kennel in baggage claim staring at me through the bars of her cage demanding immediate release. I am fumbling with the door and slow to get her leash out. I am thinking she'll give me a kiss and want some love. Nope.

Luzy leaps out of that cage. Over me. To freedom. She makes straight for the sliding glass doors leading to the street. She can't figure how the doors work so she wheels around and just runs full-out through the airport. I make a big mistake; I chase her.

She is a white husky-blur circling the baggage carousels, weaving in and out of people, and leaping over luggage. All muscle and grace and at turns slip-sliding on the glossy floors. People try to grab her but she is in full duck and weave. Level pro. No one can touch her.

Folks from our plane are enjoying the show as we circle around those damn carousels. She started her run out of stress, but as she moves she releases the anxiety and now she truly enjoys her physicality and her freedom. There is a collective "ooooh" from the crowd when I almost get her and "ah" as she leaps an upright suitcase. I am getting frustrated and embarrassed. We have completely disrupted the first floor of Anchorage International Airport. Three Alaska Airlines security workers come out and whistle commandingly, and try to triangulate on her. She winks at them and slips through.

I am worried she is going to get onto the conveyer belt or out the front doors to the street. An elderly couple is almost bowled over in the chase. I pull myself together, stop, and take a breath. Luzy disappears heading toward the Delta baggage area, and there are shouts from that direction. I can only think of one thing to do. I close my eyes and howl. It is a kind of moaning, begging, please-come-to-me howl. It's one of our calls. And... she comes running. Luzy jumps up on me and says, "Yeah! That was fun! I needed to RUN man! Do you have any food?"

Everyone applauds. No one reprimands me. Security comes up and pats me on the arm and says, "That is some dog!" A sweet girl approaches asking to pet Luzy, and others follow. Luzy preens, tail wagging. She poses for pictures.

And the Luzy Lesson for me? Be all-out YOU, wherever you are. A lot of people will love it, but more importantly, you will be true to yourself.

I quietly gather her luggage and prepare for the long midnight drive home. I love her so much.

"Who says You need to keep four paws on the ground?"

by Luzy Lesson Caption Winner
Susan Clarke,
Whitefish Montana

Stand your ground.

Take the leap. You can fly.

45

46

You get to decide what fits You.

It's time to smell the flowers.

Can you find Luzy?

She Walks Me

We are independent souls which suits us. When other dog friends join us for walks she is happy and friendly, but she goes her own way. Luzy does not follow along, she speeds ahead exploring her own trail. We enjoy our space, together.

Luzy leads and I try to keep pace as she sprints up a ridgeline, and stops to peer back at me. I nod, and she moves on. If I start to run in the woods, she delights in running faster. Somewhere ahead, out of sight, she will circle back and streak past me in a laughing blur, rejoicing in her four-legged power. Later, I jump on my paddleboard and she follows on the shoreline, running through the forest, skirting the lakes, a white streak flashing elegantly through green spruce. She marks my route, sometimes leaping in the water to swim out to the board and climb on. I am allowed to paddle her while she walks confidently around the board. She leans way out to lap water. She guesses our route between two islands and leaps into the water to make her own crossing, tumbling me into the lake while she swims ashore. We laugh.

She has taught me to dance through woods barefoot, as part of the land.

Share moments with other species.

50

You are connected to everything.

I see you
and
I love you.

I See You

Luzy hypnotized me after our first meeting, and I made the decision to borrow her for my next expedition. The plan was to skijor 150 miles from the village of Nenana to Tanana. We traveled together for 16 days into the wilderness, with temperatures dipping to 20, 30, 40 degrees below zero. We snow camped in a new, beautiful place every night and packed up every morning to venture further on our trail. I watched her and learned. I learned to talk to her without words and to listen to her. I would watch the direction of her ears and discover animals and things to be wary of on the trail. Just when I thought she was crazy-smart and intuitive, she would pull some stunt and get us all tangled in lines, causing me to fall on my face.

After 300 miles, we loaded my sled into the car, and Luzy jumped in the backseat. We started the engine and waited for the frozen car to warm. I realized I was going to be taking Luzy back to Anja's house. We would not wake up tomorrow and frolic all day long. My heart hurt. I looked over my shoulder into the backseat, and Luzy was staring back at me with this intense look... of love... with a question in her eyes. I heard quite clearly her question: Do you get it? Do you know I am coming with you? She knew I hadn't quite got it yet. I snapped this photo, I don't know why.

She watched me with this look all the way back, and when I took her to her dog yard at Anja's, she quietly got up on her dog house and sat still as I walked away.

I headed to Denver a few days later, and worked and traveled in other states for the next few months. I wanted Luzy in my life but didn't think I could swing it with all my travel. I already had three other wonderful pets.

Then came the dreams. Luzy and I would take different forms: women, men, animals. We'd be on the Yukon River (which we did three years later), or in Russia, then Italy, and Mexico. In the dreams we were always very close, but once, we just passed each other on the street, and it broke my heart. Every dream ended with us losing each other, and it would feel awful.

I began to worry about having Luzy in my life, I was afraid of the commitment and intensity. I was playing small. Until I had The Dream.

We were both polar bears roaming the land together, and it was marvelous and real and as good as a flying dream. Oh my goodness, our incredible fur coats! Human hunters came, and I turned into a human so I could tell them about us. Luzy remained a polar bear and the hunters speared her. Inconsolable, I woke up and went and got Luzy and brought her home.

Luzy is so often ahead, and waiting for me to catch up.

Many blessings to you from Luzy and me.

What is your caption?

Go to www.wendybattino.com and share your caption for this photo.
Captions will be posted on my website!

Luzy Tools

While Luzy Lessons are the pithy statements Luzy makes every day, Luzy Tools are the strategies I have learned from her to be more present in my own life. These are things I have seen her do repeatedly and I practice these myself all the time with great results, so I thought I would share them with you.

Create Friends With All Beings

Use this tool when you need some connection or want to make new friends:

~ Stand outside somewhere and say hello to yourself, shake a little or touch the earth
~ Wander aimlessly until you are called to a rock, animal, stream, plant, anything in nature and something that you feel wants to talk to you. It may or may not be a pretty thing. It could be something you are not usually attracted to, just go with it, try not to choose it with a strategic mind.
~ Sit with it and introduce yourself. Tell this thing your deep truth. Be you in front of this thing.
~ Interact through your senses, rather than your mind. Meaning you may like to talk in images or feelings or song or dance or whatever feels right to you.
~ Share as long as you want, until you feel this thing is ready to talk to YOU.
~ Then listen. Deeply. Smell, touch, (as appropriate) be with this other being.

PLAY and ENJOY! There is nothing you can do wrong here. Spend as much time as you like. I sometimes journal afterwards about what I learned, I have never seen Luzy journal, but I don't think she needs to.

Follow Your Nose Tool

For all Luzy's graceful and seemingly nonstop movement, she is constantly stopping to stand with all four feet on the earth. You will see her take in everything around her. You notice her ears erect and moving, her nose twitching, her muscles rippling, and after a few moments she knows exactly which direction she wants to go. With no further hesitation, forward she bounds with confidence and love.

Use this tool when you need some self-loving, you feel disconnected or are looking for guidance:

~ Stand wherever you are
~ Face any direction you are drawn to
~ Feel your feet, wiggle your toes to get grounded
~ Perk your ears, ripple your muscles
~ Gaze ahead, softly
~ Find one beautiful thing in front of you (There is always something! A color, a plant, a shape, whatever strikes you...)
~ Name one way that beautiful thing is like you
~ Breathe and observe, be open and playful
~ What do you notice—see, feel, hear? What stands out?
~ How does what you notice help answer your question or help you connect?
~ Move confidently in the direction of your answer.

You can employ this wherever you are in a few quick moments before a tense meeting or take as long as you like in a beautiful outdoor setting.

Your own true wisdom is always full of love.

About the Authors

I relish making a good cup of coffee on an open fire, exploring the boreal forest and tundra around my home and communing with myriad beings on the land. I am a Transformation Coach with a desire to support people in living connected with the natural world. I stir my experiences as an Archaeologist, Teacher, Executive Director, Life Coach, and Explorer into my coaching. Writing and presenting are a joy to me, and bringing people together to experience their wisdom and to heal in nature through workshops and retreats is fullfilling. I am excited to be cofounding our second Foundation with my husband, Rick, called THRIVE NATION which aims to help young adults thrive.

Luzy is an intrepid Alaskan husky who does not doubt herself. She enjoys sharing her wisdom with me and you and is keen to see humans embrace our considerable powers to do good in the world. She has one secret which only those who have met her know but she is happy to share it here: she has the softest fuzzy ears you can imagine. Luzy leaps across the tundra with her piercing blue gaze looking always ahead.

Say hello at www.wendybattino.com